A Book of
Wisdom

A Book of Wisdom

With Introductions by
Mark Fretz

Selected by
Trace Murphy

Image Books
Doubleday
New York London Toronto Sydney Auckland

AN IMAGE BOOK

PUBLISHED BY DOUBLEDAY

a division of Bantam Doubleday Dell Publishing Group, Inc.

1540 Broadway, New York, New York 10036

IMAGE, DOUBLEDAY, and the portrayal of a deer drinking from a
stream are trademarks of Doubleday, a division of Bantam
Doubleday Dell Publishing Group, Inc.

Library of Congress Cataloging-in-Publication Data
Bible. O.T. English. Selections. 1995.
A book of wisdom / with introductions by Mark Fretz;
selected by Trace Murphy.
    p.   cm.
    I. Murphy, Trace.   II. Bible. O.T. Apocrypha. Wisdom
of Solomon. English. Selections. 1995.   III. Bible. O.T.
Apocrypha. Ecclesiasticus. English. Selections. 1995.
IV. Title.
BS1403.M87   1995   95-13406
223'.05209—dc20   CIP

ISBN 0-385-47845-3
Copyright © 1995 by Doubleday, a division of Bantam
Doubleday Dell Publishing Group, Inc.
All Rights Reserved
Printed in the United States of America
First Image Books Edition: July 1995
1   3   5   7   9   10   8   6   4   2

Contents

Introduction

❧

FEW things are as universal as the quest for wisdom. Throughout life we search for meaning and direction, for happiness and contentment. The search begins at birth and never ends; we simply cross the threshold of life, leaving questions in our wake. As infants our concerns are immediate and pragmatic, but as soon as we conquer the world of words, the search turns into a series of questions—who?, what?, where?, when?, how?, and (the one that most confounds parents) why? As children, teens, young adults, throughout adulthood, and into the golden years our quest continues. Although along the way we might not be able to put our finger on it, this is a quest for wisdom.

We find wisdom in the most unusual and unexpected places. However, it is no surprise that the most widely recognized collection of wisdom literature appears in the Bible. The Bible's sages were relative latecomers to the scene of human history (ca. 1000–50 B.C.E.). But in the realm of wisdom, being late is a virtue. That which preceded Israel's sages became the stuff of their wisdom tradition. Distilled and derived from the collective fount of human experience, the biblical wisdom tradition draws upon and reflects its ancient Near Eastern environment. The stream of biblical wisdom grew in the fertile soil of Mesopotamia, Palestine, Egypt, and Greece.

Wisdom in the ancient world offers a rich source of guidance to travelers on the road of life. Clothed in catchy sayings, pithy proverbs, unforgettable stories, and pleasing poetry, wisdom satisfies the human need to know. Three themes course through this vast array of wisdom literature, providing as it were a reliable refrain to the songs of the sages. First, the wisdom of the sages appeals to ordinary people because it deals with how to live a long and fulfilling life. It relays rules for succeeding at life in the present, and has an immediacy and urgency about it. Although presented in diverse forms, ancient wisdom traditions are more akin to newspaper or magazine editorials than modern poetry or liturgy. The sayings of the sages are considered wisdom because of their relevance to everyday life. Wisdom literature can be compared to the how-to books one finds in all the bookstores.

Second, based on and directed toward human experience, wisdom literature amounts to common sense—the kinds of things everyone knows, or ought to know. These are words one might expect to hear from a grandparent or a wise and trusted friend. They grow out of a lifetime of experience, but can be learned from even the most innocent children. The sages passed on those bits of wisdom that stood the test of time. People everywhere shared a set of experiences and out of these developed an understanding of what made sense. Had biblical wisdom not made sense, it would have fallen by the wayside.

Third, related to its practicality, wisdom in the ancient world has an unapologetically ethical dimension. Thoroughly rooted in human experience, wisdom is concerned with both how to get along in life and the right and wrong of life. Ethical norms develop and generally endure over time. They reflect social sensibilities by defining what is and is not acceptable for people to do. In light of the ethical aspect of wisdom, it seems quite reasonable for ancient wisdom to be equated with law. From this perspective, wisdom amounts to the popular presentation of the do's and don'ts of life. It was important for people to be able to tell right from wrong, so they could make choices in life. It was also necessary to be able to judge the actions of others, as in disputes that are decided in a courtroom. But ultimately, wisdom literature holds up a portrait of the ideal of good character and convinces people to live their lives accordingly.

We hear these three themes in wisdom from throughout the ancient Near East. Underlying ancient Near East culture is a basic reliance on deities. While Israel's sages are part of the larger ancient Near Eastern wisdom tradition, all of which pay close attention to the divine realm, biblical wisdom literature injects spirituality on a personal level. Whether thinking of wisdom as the guide to a fulfilling life, as common sense (the laws of nature), or as the embodiment of ethical norms, the biblical sages infuse their wisdom with God's presence. Indeed, the spiritual dimension of wisdom stresses the proper relationship between people and their God. The sages are concerned with human destiny. They want people to know how best to prepare for their destinies. What ultimately happens to us after we die, claim the sages, is in the Lord's hands. God is the giver and taker of life. Likewise, God is the origin and source of all wisdom. For anyone to exclude God from his or her life is to act foolishly, both in the present and in the future. Wisdom is God's spirit, personified as a woman in the Bible. Embrace it and we find the treasures wisdom has to offer.

Wisdom amounts to knowing what leads to happiness and fulfillment, having common sense, holding ethical principles. Combined with living in proper relationship to God, these are the riches of wisdom.

A Book of
Wisdom

The Book of Job

❧

*I*N an odd way, that we know neither the identity of the author nor the date of composition of the book of Job (possibly the late sixth century B.C.E.) tells us something about the nature of its wisdom. Unique among biblical books of wisdom, Job takes an intimate look at coping with the pain and suffering of life. A tragic narrative of personal loss and unjust punishment frames Job's discussions with his friends and God, as Job desperately seeks to make sense of his experience. The dialogues convey the tension between traditional answers, which equate blessings with doing good and punishment with doing evil, and the inadequacy of the tradition in light of Job's life. On the one hand, Job's friends emphasize having the good life now and having certainty about human destiny in the future, but Job questions, ridicules, and scoffs at their naïve simplicity. On the other hand, since pat answers to life's complicated questions fail to satisfy, Job is left all alone to face God's questions. Out of the whirlwind, God poses unanswerable questions to Job that leave him speechless. Through this encounter, Job unexpectedly finds the key to wisdom in his own inability to respond to God's questions. God alone is the creator and sustainer of life, the one all-powerful being who can both give and take life. As Job realizes, both his ultimate destiny and wisdom itself are in God's hands; knowing that and living accordingly is wisdom.

❧

I know that I have a living Defender
    and that he will rise up last; on the dust
        of the earth.
After my awakening, he will set me close to
    him,
    and from my flesh I shall look on
        God.
He whom I shall see will take my part:
    my eyes will be gazing on no stranger.
    My heart sinks within me.
When you say, 'How can we confound
    him?
    What pretext can we discover against
        him?'
You yourselves had best beware the sword,
    since the wrath bursts into flame at
        wicked deeds

and then you will learn that there is
   indeed a judgement!

19:25–29

❧

Silver has its mines,
   and gold a place for refining.
Iron is extracted from the earth,
   the smelted rocks yield copper.
Man makes an end of darkness,
   to the utmost limit he digs
     the black rock in shadow dark as death.
Foreigners bore into ravines
   in unfrequented places,
     swinging suspended far from human
       beings.
That earth from which bread comes
   is ravaged underground by fire.
There, the rocks have veins of sapphire
   and their dust contains gold.

That is a path unknown to birds of prey,
   unseen by the eye of any vulture;
a path not trodden by the lordly beasts,
   where no lion ever walked.
Man attacks the flint,
   upturning mountains by their roots.
He cuts canals through the rock,
   on the watch for anything precious.
He explores the sources of rivers,
   bringing hidden things to light.
But where does Wisdom come from?
   Where is Intelligence to be found?

No human being knows the way to her,
   she is not to be found on earth where
      they live.
'She is not in me,' says the Abyss;
   'Nor here,' replies the Sea.
She cannot be bought with solid gold,
   nor paid for with any weight of silver,
nor valued against gold of Ophir,
   precious agate or sapphire.

Neither gold nor glass compares with her,
    for her, a vase of fine gold would be no
        exchange,
let alone coral or crystal:
    better go fishing for Wisdom than for
        pearls!
Topaz from Cush is worthless in
        comparison,
    and gold, even refined, is valueless.
But where does Wisdom come from?
    Where is Intelligence to be found?

She cannot be seen by any living creature,
    she is hidden from the birds of the sky.
Perdition and Death both say,
    'We have heard only rumours of her.'
God alone understands her path
    and knows where she is to be found.
(For he sees to the remotest parts of the
        earth,
    and observes all that lies under heaven.)

When he willed to give weight to the wind
  and measured out the waters with a
    gauge,
when he imposed a law on the rain
  and mapped a route for thunderclaps to
    follow,
then he saw and evaluated her,
  looked her through and through,
    assessing her.
Then he said to human beings,
  'Wisdom?—that is fear of the Lord;
  Intelligence?—avoidance of evil.'

28:1–28

The Psalms

❧

PSALMS of wisdom are sprinkled throughout the Hebrew Psalter, or book of Psalms. Peculiar phrases and forms, characteristic poetic styles, and easily identified wisdom themes distinguish certain psalms as wisdom psalms. The poetic form combined with spiritually inspiring insights offers the reader a rich fount of wisdom. The composers who followed in the footsteps of King David, Israel's most famous poet, illuminate the mundane world of common folk with the essence of divine and practical wisdom. It is not hard to imagine these poetic verses being sung to popular tunes, their repetition reinforcing the power and presence of the ancient wisdom tradition.

Psalm 1

How blessed is anyone who rejects the
   advice of the wicked
and does not take a stand in the path that
   sinners tread,
nor a seat in company with cynics,
but who delights in the law of Yahweh
and murmurs his law day and night.

Such a one is like a tree planted near
   streams;
it bears fruit in season
and its leaves never wither,
and every project succeeds.
How different the wicked, how different!

Just like chaff blown around by the wind
the wicked will not stand firm at the
    Judgement
nor sinners in the gathering of the upright.
For Yahweh watches over the path of the
    upright,
but the path of the wicked is doomed.

≈

Psalm 15

Yahweh, who can find a home in your tent,
who can dwell on your holy mountain?

Whoever lives blamelessly,
who acts uprightly,
who speaks the truth from the heart,
who keeps the tongue under control,

who does not wrong a comrade,
who casts no discredit on a neighbour,
who looks with scorn on the vile,
but honours those who fear Yahweh,

who stands by an oath at any cost,
who asks no interest on loans,
who takes no bribe to harm the innocent.
No one who so acts can ever be shaken.

ॐ

Psalm 49

Hear this, all nations,
listen, all who dwell on earth,
people high and low,
rich and poor alike!

My lips have wisdom to utter,
my heart good sense to whisper.
I listen carefully to a proverb,
I set my riddle to the music of the harp.

Why should I be afraid in times of
    trouble?
Malice dogs me and hems me in.
They trust in their wealth,
and boast of the profusion of their riches.

But no one can ever redeem himself
or pay his own ransom to God,
the price for himself is too high;
it can never be that he will live on for ever
and avoid the sight of the abyss.

For he will see the wise also die
no less than the fool and the brute,
and leave their wealth behind for others.

For ever no home but their tombs,
their dwelling-place age after age,
though they gave their name to whole
    territories.

In prosperity people lose their good sense,
they become no better than dumb animals.
So they go on in their self-assurance,
right up to the end they are content with
    their lot.

They are penned in Sheol like sheep.
Death will lead them to pasture,
and those who are honest will rule over
    them.

In the morning all trace of them will be
    gone,
Sheol will be their home.
But my soul God will ransom
from the clutches of Sheol, and will snatch
    me up.

Do not be overawed when someone gets
    rich,
and lives in ever greater splendour;
when he dies he will take nothing with
    him,
his wealth will not go down with him.

Though he pampered himself while he
    lived

—and people praise you for looking after
    yourself—
he will go to join the ranks of his
    ancestors,
who will never again see the light.

In prosperity people lose their good sense,
they become no better than dumb animals.

❧

Psalm 90

Lord, you have been our refuge
from age to age.

Before the mountains were born,
before the earth and the world came to
    birth,
from eternity to eternity you are God.

You bring human beings to the dust,
by saying, 'Return, children of Adam.'
A thousand years are to you
like a yesterday which has passed,
like a watch of the night.

You flood them with sleep
—in the morning they will be like growing
    grass:
in the morning it is blossoming and
    growing,
by evening it is withered and dry.

For we have been destroyed by your wrath,
dismayed by your anger.
You have taken note of our guilty deeds,
our secrets in the full light of your
    presence.

All our days pass under your wrath,
our lives are over like a sigh.
The span of our life is seventy years—
eighty for those who are strong—
but their whole extent is anxiety and
    trouble,
they are over in a moment and we are gone.

Who feels the power of your anger,
or who that fears you, your wrath?

Teach us to count up the days that are
    ours,
and we shall come to the heart of wisdom.
Come back, Yahweh! How long must we
    wait?
Take pity on your servants.

Each morning fill us with your faithful
    love,
we shall sing and be happy all our days;
let our joy be as long as the time that you
    afflicted us,
the years when we experienced disaster.

Show your servants the deeds you do,
let their children enjoy your splendour!
May the sweetness of the Lord be upon us,
to confirm the work we have done!

Psalm 101

I will sing of faithful love and judgement;
to you, Yahweh, will I make music.
I will go forward in the path of the
    blameless;
when will you come to me?

I will live in purity of heart,
   in my house,
I will not set before my eyes
   anything sordid.

I hate those who act crookedly;
   this has no attraction for me.
Let the perverse of heart keep away from
   me;
   the wicked I disregard.

One who secretly slanders a comrade,
    I reduce to silence;
haughty looks, proud heart,
    these I cannot tolerate.

I look to the faithful of the land
    to be my companions,
only he who walks in the path of the
    blameless
    shall be my servant.

There is no room in my house
    for anyone who practises deceit;
no liar will stand his ground
    where I can see him.

Morning after morning I reduce to silence
    all the wicked in the land,
banishing from the city of Yahweh
    all evil-doers.

ༀ

Psalm 128

How blessed are all who fear Yahweh,
  who walk in his ways!

Your own labours will yield you a living,
  happy and prosperous will you be.
Your wife a fruitful vine
  in the inner places of your house.
Your children round your table
  like shoots of an olive tree.

Such are the blessings that fall
  on those who fear Yahweh.
May Yahweh bless you from Zion!

May you see Jerusalem prosper
    all the days of your life,
and live to see your children's children!

Peace to Israel!

꿈

Psalm 133

How good, how delightful it is
    to live as brothers all together!

It is like a fine oil on the head,
    running down the beard,
running down Aaron's beard,
    onto the collar of his robes.

It is like the dew of Hermon
    falling on the heights of Zion;
for there Yahweh bestows his blessing,
    everlasting life.

The Proverbs

THIS collection of pointed, pithy sayings reflects life as it was experienced in the ancient Near East. Pragmatic, down-to-earth, and married to everyday life, these proverbs offer advice in the form of succinct sayings and admonitions. Proverbs shares the practical wisdom—common sense—of a complex, competitive, almost secular culture. God permeated Israel's sense of being to such an extent that the wisdom of this collection springs as much from divine compassion and faith as human know-how. What sets proverbs apart from other sayings is their familiarity and common usage among ordinary folk. Traditionally attributed to "Solomon son of David, king of Israel" (Prov 1:1), but

27

likely the product of court sages, the book of Proverbs (Hebrew *māšāl*) reflects centuries of human experience from Egypt to Mesopotamia.

❧

When wisdom comes into your heart
    and knowledge fills your soul with
        delight,
then prudence will be there to watch over
        you,
    and understanding will be your guardian
to keep you from the way that is evil,
    from those whose speech is deceitful,
from those who leave the paths of honesty
    to walk the roads of darkness:
those who find their joy in doing wrong,
    and their delight in deceitfulness,
whose tracks are twisted,
    and the paths that they tread crooked.

2:10—15

❧

Let faithful love and constancy never leave
    you:
  tie them round your neck,
  write them on the tablet of your heart.
Thus you will find favour and success
  in the sight of God and of people.
Trust wholeheartedly in Yahweh,
  put no faith in your own perception;
acknowledge him in every course you take,
  and he will see that your paths are
    smooth.

3:3–6

My child, hold to sound advice and
    prudence,
  never let them out of sight;
they will give life to your soul
  and beauty to your neck.
You will go on your way in safety,
  your feet will not stumble.
When you go to bed, you will not be
    afraid;
  once in bed, your sleep will be sweet.
Have no fear either of sudden terror
  or of attack mounted by wicked men,
since Yahweh will be your guarantor,
  he will keep your steps from the snare.

3:21–26

31

※

The first principle of wisdom is: acquire
    wisdom;
    at the cost of all you have, acquire
        understanding!
Hold her close, and she will make you
    great;
    embrace her, and she will be your pride;
she will provide a graceful garland for your
    head,
    bestow a crown of honour on you.

4:7–9

❧

The path of the upright is like the light of
    dawn,
    its brightness growing to the fullness of
        day;
the way of the wicked is as dark as night,
    they cannot tell the obstacles they
        stumble over.

4:18–19

❧

More than all else, keep watch over your
    heart,
    since here are the wellsprings of life.

4:23

§

Let your eyes be fixed ahead,
   your gaze be straight before you.
Let the path you tread be level
   and all your ways be firm.
Turn neither to right nor to left,
   keep your foot clear of evil.

4:25–27

§

Reprove a mocker and you attract
      contempt,
   rebuke the wicked and you attract
      dishonour.
Do not rebuke the mocker, he will hate
   you,

rebuke the wise and he will love you for
   it.
Be open with the wise, he grows wiser still,
   teach the upright, he will gain yet more.

9:7–9

❧

A slack hand brings poverty,
   but the hand of the diligent brings
      wealth.

10:4

❧

The upright is remembered with blessings,
   the name of the wicked rots away.

10:7

❧

Hatred provokes disputes,
  but love excuses all offences.

10:12

❧

Whoever abides by discipline, walks
    towards life,
  whoever ignores correction goes astray.

10:17

❧

A flood of words is never without fault;
  whoever controls the lips is wise.

10:19

❧

What the wicked fears overtakes him,
  what the upright desires comes to him as
  a present.

10:24

❧

Pride comes first; disgrace soon follows;
   with the humble is wisdom found.

11:2

❧

The uprightness of the good makes their
    way straight,
   the wicked fall by their own wickedness.

Their uprightness sets the honest free,
   the treacherous are imprisoned by their
    own desires.

11:5–6

❧

Whoever looks down on a neighbour lacks
    good sense;
  the intelligent keeps a check on the
    tongue.

11:12

❧

For want of leadership a people perishes,
  safety lies in many advisers.

11:14

❧

Faithful love brings its own reward,
   the inflexible injure their own selves.

11:17

❧

No one is made secure by wickedness,
   but nothing shakes the roots of the
      upright.

12:3

❧

The upright has compassion on his
   animals,
   but the heart of the wicked is ruthless.

12:10

❧

Whoever works his land shall have bread
   and to spare,
   but anyone who chases fantasies has no
   sense.

12:11

❧

Fools think the way they go is straight,
the wise listens to advice.

12:15

❧

The fool shows anger straightaway,
the discreet conceals dislike.

12:16

❧

To tell the truth is to further justice,
a false witness is nothing but deceit.

12:17

Thoughtless words can pierce like a sword,
but the tongue of the wise brings
healing.

12:18

Worry makes a heart heavy,
a kindly word makes it glad.

12:25

ॐ

Insolence breeds only disputes,
    wisdom lies with those who take advice.

13:10

ॐ

A sudden fortune will dwindle away,
    accumulation little by little is the way to
    riches.

13:11

❦

Hope deferred makes the heart sick,
    desire fulfilled is a tree of life.

13:12

❦

Whoever walks with the wise becomes
    wise,
    whoever mixes with fools will be ruined.

13:20

❧

There are ways that some think straight,
but they lead in the end to death.

14:12

❧

Even in laughter the heart finds sadness,
and joy makes way for sorrow.

14:13

46

❧

The simpleton believes any message,
    a person of discretion treads a careful
        path.

14:15

❧

A quick-tempered person commits rash
    acts,
but a schemer is detestable.

14:17

One who despises the needy is at fault,
   one who takes pity on the poor is
     blessed.

14:21

Hard work always yields its profit,
   idle talk brings only want.

14:23

❦

Mastery of temper is high proof of
    intelligence,
  a quick temper makes folly worse than
    ever.

14:29

❦

A mild answer turns away wrath,
  sharp words stir up anger.

15:1

Better a dish of herbs when love is there
than a fattened ox and hatred to go with
it.

15:17

Without deliberation plans come to
nothing.
Plans succeed where counsellors are
many.

15:22

A kindly glance gives joy to the heart,
  good news lends strength to the bones.

15:30

A human heart makes the plans,
  Yahweh gives the answer.

16:1

Pride goes before destruction,
  a haughty spirit before a fall.

16:18

Better be humble with the poor
   than share the booty with the proud.

16:19

Kindly words are a honeycomb,
   sweet to the taste, wholesome to the
   body.

16:24

White hairs are a crown of honour,
   they are found in the ways of
     uprightness.

16:31

A gift works like a talisman for one who
     holds it:
   it brings prosperity at every turn.

17:8

❧

Rather come on a bear robbed of her cubs
  than on a fool in his folly.

17:12

❧

As well unleash a flood as start a dispute;
  desist before the quarrel breaks out.

17:14

❧

A friend is a friend at all times,
  it is for adversity that a brother is born.

17:17

❧

A glad heart is excellent medicine,
   a depressed spirit wastes the bones away.

17:22

❧

If the fool holds his tongue, he may pass
   for wise;
   if he seals his lips, he may pass for
   intelligent.

17:28

❧

Whoever lives alone follows private whims,
and is angered by advice of any kind.

18:1

❧

A fool takes no pleasure in understanding
but only in airing an opinion.

18:2

❧

The human heart is haughty until
    destruction comes,
  before there can be glory there must be
    humility.

18:12

❧

To retort without first listening
  is both foolish and embarrassing.

18:13

❧

The language of the poor is entreaty;
  the answer of the rich harshness.

18:23

Good sense makes for self-control,
    and for pride in overlooking an offence.

19:11

It is praiseworthy to stop short of a law-
    suit;
    only a fool flies into a rage.

20:3

❧

The resources of the human heart are like
    deep waters:
    an understanding person has only to
    draw on them.

20:5

❧

Many describe themselves as people of
    faithful love,
    but who can find someone really to be
    trusted?

20:6

Do not love sleep or you will know
   poverty;
   keep your eyes open and have your fill of
   food.

20:13

Do not despoil the weak, for he is weak,
   and do not oppress the poor at the gate,
for Yahweh takes up their cause,
   and extorts the life of their extortioners.

22:22—23

༻

Do not make friends with one who gives
    way to anger;
  make no one quick-tempered a
    companion of yours,
for fear you learn such behaviour
  and in it find a snare for yourself.

22:24–25

༻

Do not wear yourself out in quest of
    wealth,
  stop applying your mind to this.
Fix your gaze on it, and it is there no
    longer,

for it is able to sprout wings
like an eagle that flies off to the sky.

23:4–5

Purchase truth—never sell it—
    wisdom, discipline, and discernment.
The father of the upright will rejoice
        indeed,
    he who fathers a wise child will have joy
        of it.
Your father and mother will be happy,
    and she who bore you joyful.

23:23–25

If you lose heart when things go wrong,
   your strength is not worth much.

24:10

To conceal a matter, this is the glory of
      God,
   to sift it thoroughly, the glory of kings.

25:2

In the presence of the king do not give
     yourself airs,
   do not take a place among the great;
better to be invited, 'Come up here',
   than be humiliated in the presence of
     the prince.

25:6—7

Clouds and wind, but no rain:
   such is anyone whose promises are
     princely but never kept.

25:14

You are pouring vinegar on a wound
    when you sing songs to a sorrowing
        heart.

25:20

An open town, and without defences:
    such is anyone who lacks self-control.

25:28

❧

Unreliable as the legs of the lame,
   so is a proverb in the mouth of fools.

26:7

❧

He takes a stray dog by the ears,
   who meddles in someone else's quarrel.

26:17

꒜

Whoever digs a pit falls into it,
    the stone comes back on him that rolls
        it.

26:27

꒜

Do not congratulate yourself about
    tomorrow,
    since you do not know what today will
        bring forth.

27:1

❧

Let someone else sing your praises, but not
    your own mouth,
    a stranger, but not your own lips.

27:2

❧

Better open reproof
    than feigned love.

27:5

≈

Trustworthy are blows from a friend,
  deceitful are kisses from a foe.

27:6

≈

Iron is sharpened by iron,
  one person is sharpened by contact with
  another.

27:17

❧

As water reflects face back to face,
 so one human heart reflects another.

27:19

❧

The wicked flees when no one is pursuing,
 the upright is bold as a lion.

28:1

❧

A country in revolt throws up many
    leaders:
  with one person wise and experienced,
    you have stability.

28:2

❧

When the upright triumph, there is great
    exultation:
  when the wicked are in the ascendant,
    people take cover.

28:12

❧

No one who conceals his sins will prosper,
   whoever confesses and renounces them
      will find mercy.

28:13

❧

Blessed the person who is never without
      fear,
   whoever hardens his heart will fall into
      distress.

28:14

❧

Anyone who reproves another
    will enjoy more favour in the end than
        the flatterer.

28:23

❧

The fool blurts out every angry feeling,
    but the wise subdues and restrains them.

29:11

Correct your child, and he will give you
     peace of mind;
   he will delight your soul.

29:17

There are three things beyond my
     comprehension,
   four, indeed, that I do not understand:
the way of an eagle through the skies,
   the way of a snake over the rock,
the way of a ship in mid-ocean,
   the way of a man with a girl.

30:18—20

Ecclesiastes

❧

QOHELET, the laconic speaker of Ecclesiastes, wrestles with the meaning of life. In the search for wisdom, he vacillates between despair and hope, futility and assurance. Skeptical Qohelet cannot affirm and repeat the simple, clear-cut wisdom sayings he has always heard, because traditional answers no longer hold up under the strain of a rapidly changing and increasingly confounding world. He begins and ends his reflections with the telling expression "vanity of vanities, all is vanity," but in between, the sage probes the universe with questions and comments about the nature of God, a healthy fear of God, happiness, wisdom, justice and injustice. Although the ancients credit Ecclesiastes to Solomon, it is more likely that Qohelet was a revered fifth-century sage and teacher.

What profit can we show for all our toil, toiling under the sun? A generation goes, a generation comes, yet the earth stands firm for ever. The sun rises, the sun sets; then to its place it speeds and there it rises. Southward goes the wind, then turns to the north; it turns and turns again; then back to its circling goes the wind. Into the sea go all the rivers, and yet the sea is never filled, and still to their goal the rivers go. All things are wearisome. No one can say that eyes have not had enough of seeing, ears their fill of hearing.

1:3–8

❧

What was, will be again,
what has been done, will be done again,
and there is nothing new under the sun!

1:9

❧

What is twisted cannot be straightened,
what is not there cannot be counted.

1:15

❦

Much wisdom, much grief;
the more knowledge, the more sorrow.

1:18

❦

There is a season for everything, a time for
  every occupation under heaven:

  A time for giving birth,
  a time for dying;
  a time for planting,
  a time for uprooting what has been
    planted.
  A time for killing,
  a time for healing;

a time for knocking down,
a time for building.
A time for tears,
a time for laughter;
a time for mourning,
a time for dancing.
A time for throwing stones away,
a time for gathering them;
a time for embracing,
a time to refrain from embracing.
A time for searching,
a time for losing;
a time for keeping,
a time for discarding.
A time for tearing,
a time for sewing;
a time for keeping silent,
a time for speaking.
A time for loving,
a time for hating;

a time for war,
a time for peace.

❧

What do people gain from the efforts they make? I contemplate the task that God gives humanity to labour at. All that he does is apt for its time; but although he has given us an awareness of the passage of time, we can grasp neither the beginning nor the end of what God does.

3:9–13

81

❧

Everything goes to the same place,
everything comes from the dust,
everything returns to the dust.

3:20

❧

I see there is no contentment for a human
being except happiness in achievement; such
is the lot of human beings. No one can tell
us what will happen after we are gone.

3:22

꙳

Better one hand full of repose
than two hands full of achievements
to chase after the wind.

4:6

꙳

Better two than one alone, since thus their
work is really rewarding. If one should fall,
the other helps him up; but what of the
person with no one to help him up when he
falls? Again: if two sleep together they keep
warm, but how can anyone keep warm alone?
Where one alone would be overcome, two
will put up resistance; and a threefold cord is
not quickly broken.

4:9–12

❧

From too much worrying comes illusion,
from too much talking, the accents of folly.

5:2

❧

True happiness lies in eating and drinking
and enjoying whatever has been achieved
under the sun, throughout the life given by
God: for this is the lot of humanity. And
whenever God gives someone riches and
property, with the ability to enjoy them and
to find contentment in work, this is a gift
from God. For such a person will hardly
notice the passing of time, so long as God
keeps his heart occupied with joy.

5:17–19

Better a good name than costly oil,
the day of death than the day of birth.
Better go to the house of mourning
than to the house of feasting;
for to this end everyone comes,
let the living take this to heart.
Better sadness than laughter:
a joyful heart may be concealed behind sad
    looks.
The heart of the wise is in the house of
    mourning,
the heart of fools in the house of gaiety.
Better attend to the reprimand of the wise
than listen to a song sung by a fool.
For like the crackling of thorns under the
    cauldron
is the laughter of fools:
and that too is futile.

But being oppressed drives a sage mad,
and a present corrupts the heart.

7:1–7

⁊⋎

Better the end of a matter than its
    beginning,
better patience than ambition.

7:8

⁊⋎

Do not be too easily exasperated, for
exasperation dwells in the heart of fools. Do
not ask why the past was better than the

present, for this is not a question prompted
by wisdom.

7:9–10

༃

Wisdom is as good as a legacy,
profitable to those who enjoy the light of
    the sun.
For as money protects, so does wisdom,
and the advantage of knowledge is this:
that wisdom bestows life on those who
    possess her.
Consider God's creation:
who, for instance, can straighten what God
    has bent?
When things are going well, enjoy yourself,
and when they are going badly, consider
    this:

God has designed the one no less than the
    other
so that we should take nothing for
    granted.
In my futile life, I have seen everything:
the upright person perishing in uprightness
and the wicked person surviving in
    wickedness.
Do not be upright to excess
and do not make yourself unduly wise:
why should you destroy yourself?
Do not be wicked to excess,
and do not be a fool:
why die before your time?
It is wise to hold on to one and not let go
    of the other,
since the godfearing will find both.

7:11–18

❧

No one on earth is sufficiently upright to do
good without ever sinning.

7:20

❧

This is another evil among those occurring
under the sun: that there should be the same
fate for everyone. The human heart, however,
is full of wickedness; folly lurks in our hearts
throughout our lives, until we end among the
dead.

But there is hope for someone still linked
      to the rest of the living:
better be a live dog than a dead lion.

9:3–4

༄

The race is not won by the speediest,
nor the battle by the champions;
it is not the wise who get food,
nor the intelligent wealth,
nor the learned favour:
chance and mischance befall them all.
We do not know when our time will come:
like fish caught in the treacherous net,
like birds caught in the snare,
just so are we all trapped by misfortune
when it suddenly overtakes us.

9:11–12

꙾

Wisdom is worth more than weapons of
   war,
but a single sin undoes a deal of good.

One dead fly can spoil the scent-maker's
   oil:
a grain of stupidity outweighs wisdom and
   glory.

9:18—10:1

꙾

Cast your bread on the water,
eventually you will recover it.

11:1

The Book of Wisdom

❧

*T*HOROUGHLY Greek in language and cultural context, the Book of Wisdom recasts Israel's wisdom tradition for Jews submerged in Hellenistic culture. First-century (B.C.E.) cosmopolitan Alexandria, Egypt, serves as the backdrop for the sage. He appraises the philosophical ideals of his Greek neighbors and their worship of animals and objects, then demonstrates the foolishness of mocking the God of the Jews. At stake is the eternal destiny of each person. Wisdom is the tree of life (3:18), rooted in the fertile soil of justice and producing the precious fruit of immortality; whereas folly grows out of injustice and ends in mortal death. Speaking in terms that his contemporaries can quickly grasp, the sage portrays wisdom as a spiritual lover to be embraced, through which people can achieve communion with the source of wisdom and life—God. Unique to the book of Wisdom is its embrace of both the Greek worldview and the religious and social history of Judaism. It weaves together spirit-centered Greek philosophy and the salvation history of God's relationship to Israel.

❧

Love uprightness you who are rulers on
    earth,
be properly disposed towards the Lord
and seek him in simplicity of heart;
for he will be found by those who do not
    put him to the test,
revealing himself to those who do not
    mistrust him.

1:1—2

❧

Wisdom will never enter the soul of a
    wrong-doer,
nor dwell in a body enslaved to sin;
for the holy spirit of instruction flees
    deceitfulness,

recoils from unintelligent thoughts,
is thwarted by the onset of vice.

1:4–5

ॐ

Beware of uttering frivolous complaints,
restrain your tongue from finding fault;
even what is said in secret has
      repercussions,
and a lying mouth deals death to the soul.

1:11

ॐ

The souls of the upright are in the hands
      of God,
and no torment can touch them.
To the unenlightened, they appeared to die,

their departure was regarded as a disaster,
their leaving us like an annihilation;
but they are at peace.
If, as it seemed to us, they suffered
        punishment,
their hope was rich with immortality;
slight was their correction, great will their
        blessings be.

3:1–5

❧

Length of days is not what makes age
        honourable,
nor number of years the true measure of
        life;
understanding, this is grey hairs,
untarnished life, this is ripe old age.

4:8–9

Wisdom is brilliant, she never fades.
By those who love her, she is readily seen,
by those who seek her, she is readily found.
She anticipates those who desire her by
          making herself known first.
Whoever gets up early to seek her will have
          no trouble
but will find her sitting at the door.
Meditating on her is understanding in its
          perfect form,
and anyone keeping awake for her will soon
          be free from care.
For she herself searches everywhere for
          those who are worthy of her,
benevolently appearing to them on their
          ways,
anticipating their every thought.

6:12–16

For Wisdom begins with the sincere desire
     for instruction,
care for instruction means loving her,
loving her means keeping her laws,
attention to her laws guarantees
     incorruptibility,
and incorruptibility brings us near to God;
the desire for Wisdom thus leads to
     sovereignty.
If then thrones and sceptres delight you,
     monarchs of the nations,
honour Wisdom, so that you may reign for
     ever.

6:17–21

For within her is a spirit intelligent, holy,
unique, manifold, subtle,
mobile, incisive, unsullied,
lucid, invulnerable, benevolent, shrewd,
irresistible, beneficent, friendly to human
       beings,
steadfast, dependable, unperturbed,
almighty, all-surveying,
penetrating all intelligent, pure
and most subtle spirits.
For Wisdom is quicker to move than any
       motion;
she is so pure, she pervades and permeates
       all things.
She is a breath of the power of God,
pure emanation of the glory of the
       Almighty:

so nothing impure can find its way into
    her.
For she is a reflection of the eternal light,
untarnished mirror of God's active power,
and image of his goodness.

7:22–26

❧

Although she is alone, she can do
    everything:
herself unchanging, she renews the world,
and, generation after generation, passing
    into holy souls,
she makes them into God's friends and
    prophets;
for God loves only those who dwell with
    Wisdom.
She is indeed more splendid than the sun,
she outshines all the constellations;

compared with light, she takes first place,
for light must yield to night,
but against Wisdom evil cannot prevail.
Strongly she reaches from one end of the
    world to the other
and she governs the whole world for its
    good.

7:27–8:1

ॐ

What human being indeed can know the
    intentions of God?
And who can comprehend the will of the
    Lord?
For the reasoning of mortals is inadequate,
our attitudes of mind unstable;
for a perishable body presses down the
    soul,
and this tent of clay weighs down the mind
    with its many cares.

It is hard enough for us to work out what
    is on earth,
laborious to know what lies within our
    reach;
who, then, can discover what is in the
    heavens?
And who could ever have known your will,
    had you not given Wisdom
and sent your holy Spirit from above?
Thus have the paths of those on earth
    been straightened
and people have been taught what pleases
    you,
and have been saved, by Wisdom.

9:13–18

❧

Wisdom delivered her servants from their ordeals.
The upright man, fleeing from the anger of his brother,
was led by her along straight paths.
She showed him the kingdom of God
and taught him the knowledge of holy things.
She brought him success in his labours
and gave him full return for all his efforts;
she stood by him against grasping and oppressive men
and she made him rich.
She preserved him from his enemies
and saved him from the traps they set for him.
In an arduous struggle she awarded him the prize,

to teach him that piety is stronger than
    all.

10:9–12

⁂

You, our God, are kind and true,
slow to anger, governing the universe with
    mercy.
Even if we sin, we are yours, since we
    acknowledge your power,
but we will not sin, knowing we count as
    yours.
To know you is indeed the perfect virtue,
and to know your power is the root of
    immortality.

15:1–3

A new attuning of the elements occurred,
as on a harp the notes may change their
        rhythm,
though all the while preserving the same
        tone;
and this is just what happened:
land animals became aquatic,
swimming ones took to the land,
fire reinforced its strength in water,
and water forgot the power of extinguishing
        it;
flames, on the other hand, did not char the
        flesh
of delicate animals that ventured into them;
nor did they melt the heavenly food
resembling ice and as easily melted.

Yes, Lord, in every way you have made
your people great and glorious;
you have never failed to help them at any
time or place.

19:18—22

Ecclesiasticus

&

$\mathcal{O}$F all the scriptural sources of wisdom, Ecclesiasticus alone presents wisdom as coming from God through the Law, or Torah. The author, a scribe named "Jesus, son of Sira" (in Hebrew "Yeshua, ben Eleazar, ben Sira"), commonly known simply as Ben Sira, finds life and therefore wisdom in God's Law and the Temple liturgy. He reflects on worldly wisdom, good behavior, social grace, and common sense, with the recurring refrain that God is the source of wisdom. In this life and especially in death, at the moment of reckoning before the seat of divine judgment, only the wisdom of the Law will balance the scales of God's justice. Ben Sira repeatedly returns to the theme of divine retribution, the union between wisdom and the Law, and fear of the Lord. Written around 190 B.C.E., Ecclesiasticus represents the culmination of Israel's search for divine wisdom.

All wisdom comes from the Lord,
  she is with him for ever.
The sands of the sea, the drops of rain,
  the days of eternity—who can count
    them?
The height of the sky, the breadth of the
    earth,
  the depth of the abyss—who can explore
    them?
Wisdom was created before everything,
  prudent understanding subsists from
    remotest ages.
For whom has the root of wisdom ever
    been uncovered?
  Her resourceful ways, who knows them?
One only is wise, terrible indeed,
  seated on his throne, the Lord.

It was he who created, inspected and
    weighed her up,
    and then poured her out on all his
    works—
as much to each living creature as he
    chose—
    bestowing her on those who love him.

☙

The rage of the wicked cannot put him in
    the right,
    for the weight of his rage is his
    downfall.
A patient person puts up with things until
    the right time comes:
    but his joy will break out in the end.
Till the time comes he keeps his thoughts
    to himself,

and many a lip will affirm how wise he
    is.

1:22–24

❧

My child, if you aspire to serve the Lord,
    prepare yourself for an ordeal.
Be sincere of heart, be steadfast,
    and do not be alarmed when disaster
        comes.
Cling to him and do not leave him,
    so that you may be honoured at the end
        of your days.
Whatever happens to you, accept it,
    and in the uncertainties of your humble
        state, be patient,
since gold is tested in the fire,
    and the chosen in the furnace of
        humiliation.

Trust him and he will uphold you,
   follow a straight path and hope in him.
You who fear the Lord, wait for his mercy;
   do not turn aside, for fear you fall.
You who fear the Lord, trust him,
   and you will not be robbed of your
      reward.
You who fear the Lord, hope for those
   good gifts of his,
   everlasting joy and mercy.

2:1–9

∾

Look at the generations of old and see:
   who ever trusted in the Lord and was
      put to shame?
Or who ever, steadfastly fearing him, was
      forsaken?
   Or who ever called to him and was
      ignored?

For the Lord is compassionate and
    merciful,
  he forgives sins and saves in the time of
    distress.

❧

Whoever respects a father expiates sins,
  whoever honours a mother is like
    someone amassing a fortune.

3:3—4

Be gentle in carrying out your business,
and you will be better loved than a
lavish giver.
The greater you are, the more humbly you
should behave,
and then you will find favour with the
Lord.

3:17–18

A stubborn heart will come to a bad end,
and whoever dallies with danger will
perish in it.
A stubborn heart is weighed down with
troubles,
the sinner heaps sin on sin.

For the disease of the proud there is no
    cure,
  since an evil growth has taken root there.
The heart of the sensible will reflect on
    parables,
  an attentive ear is the sage's dream.

3:26–29

❧

Gain the love of the community
  in the presence of the great bow your
    head.
To the poor lend an ear,
  and courteously return the greeting.
Save the oppressed from the hand of the
    oppressor,
  and do not be mean-spirited in your
    judgements.

Be like a father to the fatherless
    and as good as a husband to their
        mothers.
And you will be like a child to the Most
        High,
    who will love you more than your own
        mother does.

4:7–11

ဆ

Do not be too severe on yourself,
    do not let shame lead you to ruin.
Do not refrain from speaking when it will
        do good,
    and do not hide your wisdom;
for your wisdom is made known by what
        you say,
    your erudition by the words you utter.
Do not contradict the truth,
    rather blush for your own ignorance.

Do not be ashamed to confess your sins,
    do not struggle against the current of
      the river.

4:22–26

❧

Fight to the death for truth,
    and the Lord God will war on your side.
Do not be bold of tongue,
    yet idle and slack in deed;
do not be like a lion at home,
    or cowardly towards your servants.
Do not let your hands be outstretched to
      receive,
    yet tight-fisted when the time comes to
      give back.

4:28–31

Be steady in your convictions,
  and be a person of your word.
Be quick to listen,
  and deliberate in giving an answer.
If you understand the matter, give your
    neighbour an answer,
  if not, keep your hand over your mouth.
Both honour and disgrace come from
    talking,
  the tongue is its owner's downfall.

5:10—13

A kindly turn of speech attracts new
    friends,
    a courteous tongue invites many a
        friendly response.
Let your acquaintances be many,
    but for advisers choose one out of a
        thousand.
If you want to make a friend, take him on
    trial,
    and do not be in a hurry to trust him;
for one kind of friend is so only when it
    suits him
    but will not stand by you in your day of
        trouble.
Another kind of friend will fall out with
    you
    and to your dismay make your quarrel
        public,

and a third kind of friend will share your
    table,
  but not stand by you in your day of
    trouble:
when you are doing well he will be your
    second self,
  ordering your servants about;
but, if disaster befalls you, he will recoil
    from you
  and keep out of your way.

6:5–12

❧

A loyal friend is a powerful defence:
  whoever finds one has indeed found a
    treasure.
A loyal friend is something beyond price,
  there is no measuring his worth.
A loyal friend is the elixir of life,

and those who fear the Lord will find
  one.
Whoever fears the Lord makes true friends,
  for as a person is, so is his friend too.

6:14–17

ॐ

With all your heart honour your father,
  never forget the birthpangs of your
    mother.
Remember that you owe your birth to
  them;
  how can you repay them for what they
    have done for you?

7:27–28

❧

Do not despise anyone in old age;
　　after all, some of us too are growing old.
Do not gloat over anyone's death;
　　remember that we all have to die.

8:6–7

❧

Do not go travelling with a rash man,
　　for fear he becomes burdensome to you;
he will act as the whim takes him,
　　and you will both be ruined by his folly.

8:15

In a stranger's presence do nothing that
    should be kept secret,
  since you cannot tell what use the
    stranger will make of it.
Do not open your heart to all comers,
  nor lay claim to their good offices.

8:18–19

Do not desert an old friend;
  the new one will not be his match.
New friend, new wine;
  when it grows old, you drink it with
    pleasure.

9:10

❧

A sagacious ruler educates his people,
    and he makes his subjects understand
      order.
As the magistrate is, so will his officials be,
    as the governor is, so will be the
      inhabitants of his city.

10:1—2

❧

Do not resent your neighbour's every
    offence,
    and never act in a fit of passion.

10:6

Sovereignty passes from nation to nation
    because of injustice, arrogance and
        money.

10:8

Better the hardworking who has plenty of
    everything,
    than the pretentious at a loss for a meal.
My child, be modest in your self-esteem,
    and value yourself at your proper worth.
Who can justify one who inflicts injuries
    on himself,
    or respect one who is full of self-
        contempt?

The poor is honoured for wit,
  and the rich for wealth.
Honoured in poverty, how much the more
    in wealth!
  Dishonoured in wealth, how much the
    more in poverty!

10:27–31

❧

Wisdom enables the poor to stand erect,
  and gives to the poor a place with the
    great.

Do not praise anyone for good looks,
  nor dislike anyone for mere appearance.

Small among winged creatures is the bee
  but her produce is the sweetest of the
    sweet.

Do not grow proud when people honour
    you;
for the works of the Lord are wonderful
    but hidden from human beings.

Many monarchs have been made to sit on
    the ground,
    and the person nobody thought of has
    worn the crown.
Many influential people have been utterly
    disgraced,
    and prominent people have fallen into
    the power of others.

11:1–6

≈

My child, do not take on a great amount
    of business;
  if you multiply your interests, you are
    bound to suffer for it;
hurry as fast as you can, yet you will never
    arrive,
  nor will you escape by running away.
Some people work very hard at top speed,
  only to find themselves falling further
    behind.

11:10—11

❧

Good and bad, life and death,
  poverty and wealth, all come from the
    Lord.

11:14

❧

A moment's adversity, and pleasures are
    forgotten;
  in a person's last hour his deeds will
    stand revealed.
Call no one fortunate before his death;
  it is by his end that someone will be
    known.

11:27–28

꩜

In prosperity you cannot always tell a true
  friend,
    but in adversity you cannot mistake an
    enemy.
When someone is doing well that person's
    enemies are sad,
    when someone is doing badly, even a
    friend will keep at a distance.
Do not ever trust an enemy;
    as bronze tarnishes, so does an enemy's
    malice.
Even if he behaves humbly and comes
    bowing and scraping,
    maintain your reserve and be on your
    guard against him.

12:8–11

Who feels sorry for a snake-charmer bitten
   by a snake,
   or for those who take risks with savage
   animals?—
just so for one who consorts with a sinner,
   and becomes an accomplice in his sins.
He will stay with you for a while,
   but if you once give way he will press
   his advantage.
An enemy may have sweetness on his lips,
   and in his heart a scheme to throw you
   into the ditch.
An enemy may have tears in his eyes,
   but if he gets a chance there can never
   be too much blood for him.
If you meet with misfortune, you will find
   him there before you,

and, pretending to help you, he will trip
    you up.
He will wag his head and clap his hands,
    he will whisper a lot and his expression
    will change.

12:13–18

❧

When an influential person invites you,
    show reluctance,
    and he will press his invitation all the
    more.

Do not thrust yourself forward, in case you
    are pushed aside,
    but do not stand aloof, or you will be
    overlooked.

13:9–10

❧

Blessed is anyone who has not sinned in
    speech
  and who needs feel no remorse for sins.
Blessed is anyone whose conscience does
    not reproach him
  and who has never given up hope.

14:1–2

❧

My child, treat yourself as well as you can
    afford,
  and bring worthy offerings to the Lord.
Remember that death will not delay,
  and that you have never seen Sheol's
    contract.

Be kind to your friend before you die,
　　treat him as generously as you can
　　　　afford.
Do not refuse yourself the good things of
　　　　today,
　　do not let your share of what is lawfully
　　　　desired pass you by.
Will you not have to leave your fortune to
　　　　another,
　　and the fruit of your labour to be
　　　　divided by lot?
Give and receive, enjoy yourself—
　　there are no pleasures to be found in
　　　　Sheol.
Like clothes, every body will wear out,
　　the age-old law is, 'Everyone must die.'
Like foliage growing on a bushy tree,
　　some leaves falling, others growing,
so are the generations of flesh and blood:
　　one dies, another is born.

Every achievement rots away and perishes,
   and with it goes its author.

14:11–19

ॐ

Blessed is anyone who meditates on
      wisdom
   and reasons with intelligence,
who studies her ways in his heart
   and ponders her secrets.

14:20–21

Does not dew relieve the heat?
   In the same way a word is worth more
      than a gift.
Why surely, a word is better than a good
      present,
   but a generous person is ready with
      both.

18:16–17

Learn before you speak,
   take care of yourself before you fall ill.
Examine yourself before judgement comes,
   and on the day of visitation you will be
      acquitted.

Humble yourself before you fall ill,
   repent as soon as the sin is committed.
Let nothing prevent your discharging a vow
      in good time,
   and do not wait till death to set matters
   right.

18:19–22

                          ᢒᵛ

Do not be governed by your passions,
   restrain your desires.
If you allow yourself to satisfy your desires,
   this will make you the laughing-stock of
      your enemies.
Do not indulge in luxurious living,
   do not get involved in such society.

Do not beggar yourself by banqueting on
        credit
    when there is nothing in your pocket.

                                    18:30–33

                        ⤳

Never repeat what you are told
    and you will come to no harm;
whether to friend or foe, do not talk about
        it,
    unless it would be sinful not to, do not
        reveal it;
you would be heard out, then mistrusted,
    and in due course you would be hated.
Have you heard something? Let it die with
        you.
    Courage! It will not burst you!
A fool will suffer birthpangs over a piece
        of news,
    like a woman labouring with child.

Like an arrow stuck in the flesh of the
    thigh,
  so is a piece of news inside a fool.

19:7–12

❧

Throw stones at birds and you scare them
    away,
  reproach a friend and you destroy a
    friendship.

22:20

❧

Win your neighbour's confidence when he
    is poor,
  so that you may enjoy his later good
    fortune with him;

stand by him in times of trouble,
   in order to have your share when he
      comes into a legacy.

22:23

~

Do not get into the habit of using coarse
   and foul language
since this involves sinful words.
Remember your father and mother
   when you are sitting with the great,
for fear you forget yourself in their
      presence
   and behave like a fool,
and then wish you had not been born
   and curse the day of your birth.

23:13–14

༇

There are three things my soul delights in,
   and which are delightful to God and to
      all people:
concord between brothers, friendship
      between neighbours,
   and a wife and husband who live happily
      together.

There are three sorts of people my soul
      hates,
   and whose existence I consider an
      outrage:
the poor swollen with pride, the rich who
      is a liar
   and an adulterous old man who has no
      sense.

25:1–2

❧

If you have gathered nothing in your youth,
  how can you find anything in your old
    age?
How fine a thing: sound judgement with
  grey hairs,
    and for greybeards to know how to
    advise!
How fine a thing: wisdom in the aged,
  and considered advice coming from
    people of distinction!

25:3–5

In a shaken sieve the rubbish is left behind,
   so too the defects of a person appear in
     speech.
The kiln tests the work of the potter,
   the test of a person is in conversation.
The orchard where the tree grows is judged
     by its fruit,
   similarly words betray what a person
     feels.
Do not praise anyone who has not yet
     spoken,
   since this is where people are tested.

27:4–7

❧

If you pursue virtue, you will attain it
  and put it on like a festal gown.
Birds consort with their kind,
  truth comes home to those who practise
    it.
The lion lies in wait for its prey,
  so does sin for those who do wrong.

27:8–10

❧

Avoid quarrelling and you will sin less;
  for the hot-tempered provokes quarrels,
a sinner sows trouble between friends,
  introducing discord among the peaceful.
The way a fire burns depends on its fuel,

a quarrel spreads in proportion to its
   violence;
a man's rage depends on his strength,
   his fury grows fiercer in proportion to
   his wealth.

28:8–10

&

Lend to your neighbour in his time of
   need,
   and in your turn repay your neighbour
   on time.
Be as good as your word and keep faith
   with him,
   and you will find your needs met every
   time.

29:2–3

❦

The first thing in life is water, and bread,
     and clothing,
   and a house for the sake of privacy.
Better the life of the poor under a roof of
     planks,
   than lavish fare in somebody else's house.
Whether you have little or much, be
     content with it,
   and you will not hear your household
     complaining.

                              29:21–23

༝

Better be poor if healthy and fit
    than rich if tormented in body.
Health and strength are better than any
        gold,
    a robust body than untold wealth.
No riches can outweigh bodily health,
    no enjoyment surpass a cheerful heart.

30:14–16

༝

Do not abandon yourself to sorrow,
    do not torment yourself with brooding.
Gladness of heart is life to anyone,
    joy is what gives length of days.
Give your cares the slip, console your heart,
    chase sorrow far away;

for sorrow has been the ruin of many,
  and is no use to anybody.

30:21–23

❧

Jealousy and anger shorten your days,
  and worry brings premature old age.
A genial heart makes a good trencherman,
  someone who enjoys a good meal.

30:24–25

❧

Wine gives life
  if drunk in moderation.
What is life worth without wine?
  It came into being to make people
    happy.

Drunk at the right time and in the right
    amount,
  wine makes for a glad heart and a
    cheerful mind.
Bitterness of soul comes of wine drunk to
    excess
  out of temper or bravado.

31:27–29

ॐ

A much travelled man knows many things,
  and a man of great experience will talk
    sound sense.

Someone who has never had his trials
    knows little;
  but the travelled man is master of every
    situation.

34:9–10

※

The stomach takes in all kinds of food,
    but some foods are better than others.
As the palate discerns the flavour of game,
    so a shrewd listener detects lying words.
A perverse character causes depression in
        others;
    it needs experience to know how to
    repay such a one.

36:18–20

※

Any adviser will offer advice,
    but some are governed by self-interest.
Beware of someone who offers advice;
    first find out what he wants himself—

since his advice coincides with his own
        interest—
    in case he has designs on you
and tells you, 'You are on the right road,'
    but stands well clear to see what will
        happen to you.

37:7–9

ૐ

Stick to the advice your own heart gives
        you,
    no one can be truer to you than that;
since a person's soul often gives a clearer
        warning
    than seven watchmen perched on a
        watchtower.

37:13–14

During your life, my child, see what suits
    your constitution,
    do not give it what you find disagrees
    with it;
for not everything is good for everybody,
    nor does everybody like everything.
Do not be insatiable for any delicacy,
    do not be greedy for food,
for over-eating leads to illness
    and excess leads to liver-attacks.
Many people have died from over-eating;
    control yourself, and so prolong your
    life.

37:21–31

Shed tears over the dead,
   lament for the dead to show your
      sorrow,
then bury the body with due ceremony
   and do not fail to honour the grave.
Weep bitterly, beat your breast,
   observe the mourning the dead deserves
for a day or two, to avoid censorious
      comment,
   and then be comforted in your sorrow;
for grief can lead to death,
   a grief-stricken heart loses all energy.
In affliction sorrow persists,
   a life of grief is hard to bear.
Do not abandon your heart to grief,
   drive it away, bear your own end in
      mind.

Do not forget, there is no coming back;
 you cannot help the dead, and you will
  harm yourself.
'Remember my doom, since it will be yours
  too;
 I yesterday, you today!'
Once the dead are laid to rest, let their
  memory rest,
 do not fret for them, once their spirit
  departs.

38:16–23

*

For a person of private means and one
        who works hard,
    life is pleasant,
    better off than either, one who finds a
        treasure.

40:18

*

When I was still a youth, before I went
        travelling,
    in my prayers I asked outright for
        wisdom.
Outside the sanctuary I would pray for her,
    and to the last I shall continue to seek
        her.

From her blossoming to the ripening of her
   grape
   my heart has taken its delight in her.
My foot has pursued a straight path,
   I have sought her ever since my youth.
By bowing my ear a little, I have received
   her,
   and have found much instruction.
Thanks to her I have advanced;
   glory be to him who has given me
   wisdom!
For I was determined to put her into
   practice,
   have earnestly pursued the good, and
   shall not be put to shame.
My soul has fought to possess her,
   I have been scrupulous in keeping the
   Law;
I have stretched out my hands to heaven
   and bewailed how little I knew of her;
I have directed my soul towards her,
   and in purity I have found her;

having my heart fixed on her from the
outset,
I shall never be deserted;
my very core having yearned to discover
her,
I have now acquired a good possession.
In reward the Lord has given me a tongue
with which I shall sing his praises.
Come close to me, you ignorant,
take your place in my school.
Why complain about lacking these things
when your souls are so thirsty for them?
I have opened my mouth, I have said:
'Buy her without money,
put your necks under her yoke,
let your souls receive instruction,
she is near, within your reach.'
See for yourselves: how slight my efforts
have been
to win so much peace.
Buy instruction with a large sum of silver,
thanks to her you will gain much gold.

May your souls rejoice in the mercy of the
Lord,
    may you never be ashamed of praising
    him.
Do your work before the appointed time
    and at the appointed time he will give
    you your reward.

51:13–30